About this book

Myths and legends portray the wolf as a savage and cruel man-eater, hunting in large, vicious packs. In this delightful book, Ewan Clarkson draws on his own experience and knowledge of wolves to show how unjust this portrait is. Basing his account on a year in the life of a wolf cub, from its first tottering steps into the dangers of the North American forest, he reveals how wolves really live.

About the author

Ewan Clarkson, well-known for his many books and articles on natural history, has also had seven years veterinary experience and worked as a zoo keeper and mink farmer. His travels throughout Britain and North America studying wildlife have provided him with material for various novels based on the lives of animals. In search of wolves, he explored the remoter corners of Wisconsin, Michigan and Minnesota, camping, canoeing and snowshoeing through the north woods.

Sir Maurice Yonge, Consultant Editor to the series, is Honorary Fellow in Zoology in the University of Edinburgh.

Animals of the World

First published in 1980 by
Wayland Publishers Limited
49 Lansdowne Place, Hove
East Sussex, BN3 1HF, England

Typesetting in the U.K. by Granada Graphics
Printed in Italy by G. Canale & C. S.p.A., Turin

First published in the United States of America by
Raintree Publishers Limited, 1980

Library of Congress Cataloging in Publication Data

Clarkson, Ewan
  Wolves

  (Animals of the World)
  Includes index
  SUMMARY: Introduces the characteristics, habits,
and environment of timberwolves.
    1. Wolves —Juvenile literature. [1. Wolves]
I. Title.   II. Series.
QL737.C22C58   599'.74442   79-19227
ISBN 0-8172-1089-X lib. bdg.

Animals of the World
Consultant Editor: Sir Maurice Yonge CBE FRS

Wolves

Ewan Clarkson

RAINTREE CHILDRENS BOOKS
Milwaukee • Toronto • Melbourne • London

599
CLA

82536

Spring comes late to the woods of North America, so it was mid-June before the little wolf took a few tottering steps to the mouth of the den for his first look at the world. The evening air was moist and warm, and birdsong mingled with the distant mutter of thunder. The little wolf would have ventured further, but his mother lay on guard across the entrance and barred his way. So on this first evening he had to be content to stand and stare, and sniff the exciting scents carried by the breeze.

Earlier in the year, in March, when the lakes were frozen hard and snow lay deep in the woods, his mother had enjoyed a brief honeymoon with her life-long mate. Then nine weeks later in May, as the ice broke and the snow melted away, she had come to this gravel bank to dig her den. That had been four weeks ago. There in the darkness, naked, blind and deaf, the little wolf had been born. He had been the first to arrive of a litter of four. Already he was bigger and heavier. Barring accidents, he would survive and grow strong.

For the next four weeks he had little to do but sleep, drink the rich milk his mother provided, and play. For hours he played games

of pounce and tag with the other cubs, and
when they wearied, he turned to his mother.
His father came to visit sometimes, and he
played with the cub too. Wolves are the most
tolerant of parents, enduring any amount of
ear-biting, scratching and tail pulling. When
at last even his parents grew tired of his
torment, there were older brothers and sisters,
and even an aunt, to "baby sit" for a while.
This play was important to the little wolf, de-
veloping his puny muscles, strengthening his

legs and jaws. Already too, in his play, he was learning how to spring, and worry his prey.

His parents were Timber Wolves. Their territory lay in the vast forests of North America and Canada. Further north, others of his kind, known as tundra wolves, preyed on the great herds of caribou that roamed the barren lands of the Arctic. Once wolves were to be found throughout the North American continent, and packs of wolves preyed on the buffalo that wandered the prairies. Now the prairies have gone, and so, from most of the United States, have the wolves. A few remain, in Minnesota and Michigan, and perhaps in Montana.

In almost every way the Timber Wolf resembles the European Wolf. Indeed the ancestors of the Timber Wolf probably crossed from Europe to North America, following game herds from Siberia. They would have crossed the land bridge formed by the Ice Age, over what is now the Bering Straits. Similarly, wolves migrated into England from Europe, crossing the marshy plain that is now the North Sea. A wolf pack transported from Canada to Siberia would feel perfectly at home.

Other species of wolf still survive throughout the world. The Red Wolf lives in Texas. In India there is a small, gray, short-haired wolf known as the Pale-Footed Wolf. In Brazil and the Argentine there is the Red Maned Wolf, looking like a gigantic fox with a very short body and elongated legs. Dingoes, Jackals and Dholes are also related to the wolf.

The little wolf's father was a handsome silver gray, with a darker mane. He weighed as much as a small man, with his shoulder as high as a man's waist. His mother was smaller and her pelt was more sandy. Wolves' individual coats range from jet black to pure

white, but most have an overall tinge of gray.

At first glance the little wolf's father looked like a big Alsatian dog, but there were many differences. His legs were longer and slimmer, his hindquarters rounder and more muscular, so that he seemed taller at the rump than at the shoulder. His head was different too, larger and more rounded, his eyes set further apart. His cheeks bulged with massive jaw muscles, more powerful than those of a dog. They could crush bone, or slash through thick hide. His gait, when he moved, was nervous and springy, again unlike that of a dog. Even so, wolves and dogs can interbreed. Early settlers in North America discovered that if a sheepdog bitch in season was tethered

out in the open, male wolves would mate with her. The offspring were big and strong, willing workers at the sled, but they remained timid and shy with people.

The little wolf would never have to pull a sled, but he too would have to grow big and strong in order to run with the pack. Perhaps one day he would lead the pack, like his father. So he worked at his exercises and grew fast.

About this time his mother moved the whole litter to another den, about a mile away, carrying each cub singly in her jaws. This den was bigger and roomier than the old one, which had grown cramped and stuffy. It lay

inside the root of a giant pine, which had fallen during the previous winter. The hollow left where the roots had been torn out of the ground made an ideal safe playground for the cubs, with steep banks over which they could not climb.

Now their mother began to wean the cubs. Every time the pack killed she brought meat back to the den, carrying the meat in her stomach and regurgitating it in front of the hungry cubs. At first this sounds like a rather nasty habit, but it had its advantages. If she had carried the meat in her mouth it would have been covered in dust, sand and pine needles, from trailing on the ground. Furthermore, in dragging meat back to the den, she would have left a trail for enemies — wolverine, bear, lynx or fisher — any of which would take an unguarded wolf cub. As things were, the meat arrived fresh, warm, undigested and clean, and the whereabouts of the den remained a secret. Besides, it was very handy for the she-wolf to carry a built-in shopping basket!

Soon other members of the pack also brought in meat for the cubs. At last they were grown enough to go on short hunts with the adults, pouncing on mice and chasing snowshoe hares. Sometimes danger threatened, as when the little wolf met a porcupine. The cub would have liked to play, but his mother drove him away. She knew that the porcupine's quills could cause lameness, blindness and even death.

One of the female cubs was carried off by a bald eagle when she strayed too far from the pack. So now the litter was reduced to three. Bald eagles normally eat fish, but they do not mind a little fresh red meat now and then, or even carrion.

Deaths among young wolves are not uncommon, but once a wolf is fully grown it would need to be very careless to get killed. The slashing hoofs of a moose, backed by its great weight of muscle and bone, would reduce a wolf to mere rags of skin if the wolf was not quick on its feet. A grizzly bear, like the one below, would kill a wolf, if the wolf did not keep out of its way. Humans, however, have always been the wolf's greatest enemy.

Before the first page of history came to be written, people had learned to hate and fear the wolf that came by night and robbed them of their sheep and goats. Perhaps, even earlier in time, they had come to recognize the wolf as a rival. Before they had discovered how to domesticate animals, humans had also been

hunters. They had killed large animals by surrounding them and clubbing them to death with sticks and stones, or stampeding them over a cliff.

In those days people hunted in packs. So did the wolf. Humans hunted big game. So did the wolf, and the wolf was a better hunter. It must have been hard for early man, often reduced to near starvation, to see his greatest rival faring better. So people learned to throw stones, to drive the wolf away, but — perhaps because his paws were the wrong shape — the wolf

never learned to throw them back. Instead, the wolf kept out of people's way, and so, as well as being considered savage and cruel, the wolf got the reputation of being cunning and cowardly, slinking through the shadows and only attacking defenceless prey.

Perhaps because of these fears, people exaggerated tales of the wolf's ferocity, and heightened their children's natural fears with fairy stories like "Little Red Riding Hood", and fables about werewolves. There are many legends about people on sleds being pursued over the snow by packs of forty or fifty howling wolves.

All of which is rather unfair to the wolf. In North America, at least, not one single proven record exists of a wolf killing a human being. True, if a very old person, or a baby, were abandoned in the forest, wolves might eat them. If wolves didn't, something else would. Also, wolves did frequent battlegrounds to feed on the corpses, and no doubt they ate the bodies of Indians who had died of smallpox. Meat was meat to them, whether the corpse wore antlers, moccasins, or a Roman breastplate. In fact, the wolves were doing a useful waste-disposal job. As for packs of forty or fifty wolves . . . four or five would be nearer the truth!

If humans feared the wolf, the wolf certainly feared humans, avoiding them whenever possible. I have stood alone on the ice of a frozen lake in the dark of a winter's night, and no wolf came near, let alone molested me. I have howled to a wolf pack only a short distance away, and the pack has howled back, but remained hidden. Yet I was unarmed, save for a penknife. We need not fear wolves.

Yet wolves have plenty to fear from us. No method of cutting down the number of wolves has been considered too cruel to use.

Perhaps the most fiendish and widespread slaughter began around 1850, at the time of the California gold rush, when a cargo of the poison strychnine was shipped to San Francisco. From there its use spread throughout North America, as wolf hunters followed the great herds of buffalo over the prairie, shooting them and lacing the carcasses with strychnine. Strychnine poisoning leads to a horribly painful death, yet thousands of wolves were killed this way each winter for their skins. At one time the United States government was supplying the Russian army with

wolf skins! Wolf hunters led a harsh and dangerous life, because the strychnine poisoned the grass of the prairie, and the ponies belonging to the Indians sickened and died after eating it. So the Indians killed the wolf hunters and took their horses.

When all the buffalo were gone, the cowboys with their cattle took over the prairie. Each cowboy carried a supply of strychnine and, whenever a steer died from whatever cause, it was poisoned. This practice not only killed wolves but any other animal which happened to feed on the carcass — cougar, wolverine, badger, kit fox, hawk or eagle. Even today ranchers and farmers argue against any preservation of the wolf.

Only in the great forests to the north are wolves barely tolerated. Here they help the forester by keeping down the numbers of browsing animals which, left unchecked, would damage the trees. This is a sensible idea, for wolves make excellent game wardens, and furthermore they need no wages, no transport, and they don't even need to be given a rifle.

It was late summer before our young wolf did his first tour of duty with the pack. The

pack was a family group which, with the youngsters, now numbered eight. The rains had ceased and the forests were tinder dry. Hot sun burned down by day, and the nights were crisp and cold. One chilly dawn the pack came upon a cow moose and her calf. The pack leader separated the mother from her young one and kept the enraged animal occupied as the rest of the pack pulled the calf down.

When the calf was dead the mother ran off. The pack breakfasted, until there was nothing left of the calf save the skull and bits of bone and hair. At first sight it seems senseless and cruelly wasteful to rob a moose of its calf. All winter the cow had carried the calf inside her, nourishing it with what food she could find in the snowy wastes, and finally giving birth in late spring. Now, a few months later, the calf was dead, and all that effort and self-sacrifice wasted.

Yet you must remember that the forest does not exist to serve the moose. The moose exists to serve the forest, and what the forest gives, it claims back in time. Every time the moose fed, it took minerals and salts from the forest to make bones and blood and muscle. Now, via the digestive systems of the wolves, the forest was claiming its wealth back, to convert into other forms of life.

The moose calf was unlucky. Had it survived a few months longer it would have grown too rough and tough for the wolves to tackle. Then the wolves would have had to wait until the moose got diseased, or

weakened by the parasites that would eventually infest its lungs and heart. Before that time the wolf pack would see that moose many times, and chase it to test it out. The wolves would know when the strength of the moose was beginning to fail. Then they would attack in earnest.

Often the wolf pack fed well. Often they went hungry, sometimes for days. The young wolf learned to travel up to thirty miles a day, swinging along at a steady five miles an hour over a territory of about a hundred square

miles. The pack might test ten or a dozen victims before making a kill. Imagine a golfer only hitting one ball in ten, or a duck shooter using a dozen shots to get one bird! He'd pretty soon get discouraged. Not so the wolf pack. They knew time was on their side. When they fed they fed well, the adults eating up to 9 kg. (20 lb.) of meat at a single sitting. They also ate hide and bone and entrails, so there was usually little left for the ravens that always followed the pack.

Sometimes the pack killed when they were

38

not particularly hungry; then they abandoned the carcass before it was half eaten. Today, human deer hunters coming on such a kill proclaim loudly about what they call "waste," and urge that wolves should be exterminated. They forget that nothing is wasted in the wild, and if the wolves don't eat the carcass, something else will — a wolverine, a fox, an eagle or a bear. Even a porcupine will gnaw at the bones. At times even humans, lost and starving in the wilderness, have had their lives saved by eating an abandoned wolf kill.

The brief summer passed. The leaves of the aspen withered and died, the birch trees turned golden in the sunlight, and the air was

filled with the clamor of wild geese flying south. In the morning the shores of the lake were rimmed with ice. The young wolf had long since left the den. He and his brother and sister ran with the pack.

With the coming of winter his coat was thick and glossy, and he reached almost half his full-grown weight. However hard the winter, he was now big enough, and strong enough, to survive until spring. Yet without the pack he could not hope to survive. His father and mother were the leaders; each member of the pack had its rank and status. He

was third from the bottom! Yet he was learning all the time, watching his father hang from the nose of a deer in order to pull it to the ground, or noting the sideways spring at the hind-quarters of a moose, and the terrible snapping bite that cut the hamstring of the victim, and crippled it so it could not run.

He also learned the body language of the pack, and was quick to apologize when he had behaved wrongly. Older wolves expected to be treated with respect, and he also had to watch his manners at the table. If he didn't, he got nipped – and it hurt!

It is the nature of the wolf to be eternally restless. So, even when the pack slept after a kill, the first wolf to wake would go round the others rousing each one in turn. Sometimes one member would give vent to his feelings by howling. When this happened every other member of the pack would join in, their voices blending in harmony, striving to strike the same note. Even the young wolf joined in with excited yaps and yelps, although he had not yet learned to howl. Howling seems to help bond the pack together. Certainly, all wolves enjoy a good sing.

The young wolf greeted the first snowfalls

with fascination and delight, playing puppy-like in the soft white drifts. Soon, however, he learned that snow was not always fun, for when it lay soft and fluffy he sank chest deep into it with every bound. This made hunting difficult, so he was happier when a hard crust froze on the surface. Then the pack could run light-footed over the crust. But heavier animals broke through the snow, and this made even full-grown moose easier to catch and kill.

At other times the ice crust would be so thin
that he himself broke through at every step;
then he had to be careful that he did not cut his
legs. Sometimes the snow fell wet and froze
between his pads. Then he had to learn to bite
the ice free, or it would lame him. There was a
lot to learn about snow.

His thick pelt insulated him from the cold.
He learned to sleep curled in a ball, his pads
turned upwards and tucked into his body to

guard against frostbite. The tip of his nose, another vulnerable spot, was kept covered with his bushy tail.

Now the deer were gathering in twos and threes in the cedar swamps, and sometimes the snow fell so thickly that it walled them in. Then they were easy to catch. At other times they were impossible to find. The beavers were safe under the ice until the spring, as were the muskrats. Snowshoe hares were fleet of foot, and provided very little meat when caught.

Birds, such as the ptarmigan and grouse,

were little more than a mouthful of feathers. Since each wolf in the pack needed the equivalent of twenty-four deer a year to survive, hunting occupied most of their time.

Even so, sometimes a whole week passed without the pack making a kill. Once an old bull moose, though severely wounded, fought them off so valiantly that the pack had to wait twenty-four hours until the bull's wounds

stiffened so much that they crippled him. Then, weak from loss of blood, the moose fell in the snow.

Wolves cannot kill large prey outright. They have to wait for shock and pain and loss of blood to bring death. Though this seems cruel, death from starvation or disease is a longer form of suffering. Left to themselves, moose and deer populations would soon become so great that all the available browse would be eaten. So in winter large numbers of animals would starve. The wolves keep these populations under control.

The long winter passed. At last the arrival of the bald eagles at their nesting site heralded the coming of spring. The sap began to run in the maples, and the sun grew warmer. Then suddenly the ice went from the lakes, the snow honeycombed, and for a fortnight the pack had to endure the misery of the thaw. A warm, drying wind eventually came. The beavers emerged from hibernation, some of them providing a welcome change of diet for the pack.

A pair of nesting loons arrived at the lake. One evening their calls echoed over the surrounding forest. The young wolf listened a

while, then sat down on his haunches and raised his muzzle high. For the first time in his life he managed the full-throated howl of his kind. Though another two years would pass before he reached maturity, he had survived the most testing time of his life. With luck he would live on, another ten or a dozen years, a loyal servant of the wilderness.

Glossary

BROWSE   Twigs, young shoots and leaves of trees, eaten by some animals.

CARRION   Remains of a dead animal, usually decaying.

CEDAR   Eastern white cedar, an evergreen growing in Canada and eastern United States, favorite winter food of deer.

COUGAR   Puma, a big cat native to North America.

DOMESTICATE   Make tame enough to manage and handle. All farm animals are domesticated.

FISHER   Large black weasel, also known as the sable, found in northern Europe and America.

GLACIER   River of ice. Though slow moving, often huge and powerful.

HAMSTRING   Large tendon at back of leg. If cut, the leg is useless.

LOON   Large diving bird wintering in the Arctic, and migrating to North America to breed.

MATURITY   Full development.

MOCCASIN   Soft shoe, usually made from moosehide.

MUSKRAT   Small, beaver-like rodent, living in swamps and making a little domed house of reeds and grass.

PARASITE   Animal living in or on another larger animal and taking food from it. Fleas, lice, and tapeworms are all parasites.

PRAIRIE   Great open plains covered in grassland, which once covered thousands of square miles. Now mostly farmed for wheat.

REGURGITATION   The act of bringing up undigested food from the stomach for the purpose of feeding young.

SNOWSHOE HARE   A kind of hare, so called because it has large feet to carry it over the snow.

STRYCHNINE   Poison made from the seed of the Nux Vomica plant. Death from this poison is violent and painful.

TERRITORY   Area of land used by a pack as its own hunting ground. Wolves will fight to protect their territory, but prefer to mark the boundaries with scent as a warning to other packs.

TUNDRA   Land in the Arctic where the subsoil is permanently frozen. Only the hardiest lichens and plants can grow there.

WEREWOLF   Human being who was thought to have turned into a wolf. There was a very rare form of leprosy in which the unfortunate victim grew to look like a wolf, and craved raw flesh. This may be how the legends of werewolves started.

WOLVERINE   The largest of the weasel family, bigger than a badger.

Further reading

Burton, Maurice and Burton, Robert, editors. *The New International Wildlife Encyclopedia*. 21 vols. Milwaukee: Purnell Reference Books, 1980.

Clarkson, Ewan. *Wolf Country: A Wilderness Pilgrimage*. New York: Dutton, 1975.

Crisler, Lois. *Captive Wild*. Harper and Row, 1968.

Fiennes, Richard. *The Order of Wolves*. Indianapolis: Bobbs-Merrill, 1976.

Lopez, Barry Holstun. *Of Wolves and Men*. New York: Scribner, 1978.

Mech, L. David. *The Wolf; the Ecology and Behavior of an Endangered Species*. Garden City, New York: Natural History Press, 1970.

Picture acknowledgments

Endpapers and photographs on pages 3, 4, 16, 34 and 46 by Picturepoint, London. All other photographs from Bruce Coleman Limited, by the following photographers: Bill Brooks, 37; John M. Burnley, 21, 25, 36; Bob and Clara Calhoun, 22-3; Bruce Coleman, 9; Udo Hirsch, front and back cover, 1, 6, 10, 12-13, 27, 30, 40, 41; Wayne Lankinen, 24; George Laycock, 49; Fritz Prenzel, 11; Hans Reinhard, 19; Dick Robinson, 5, 14-15, 17; Leonard Lee Rue, 8, 18, 26; James Simon, 28-9, 44-5; Stouffer Productions, 20, 32, 35, 39; Norman Tomalin, 7; Joe Van Wormer, 33, 38, 47.

Index